Double Self-Portrait

Also by James Lindsay

Ekphrasis! Ekphrasis!

Our Inland Sea

Double Self-Portrait

James Lindsay

Buckrider Books

Buckrider Books is an imprint of Wolsak and Wynn Publishers.
Cover and interior design: Jared Shapiro
Cover Image: Jeff Wall
Author photograph: Colin Medley
Typeset in Crimson Text
Printed by Coach House Printing Company Toronto, Canada

The publisher gratefully acknowledges the support of the Ontario Arts
Council, the Canada Council for the Arts and the Government of Canada.

Buckrider Books
280 James Street North
Hamilton, ON
Canada L8R 2L3

Library and Archives Canada Cataloguing in Publication

Title: Double self-portrait / James Lindsay.
Names: Lindsay, James, 1982- author.
Description: Poems.
Identifiers: Canadiana 2020016628X | ISBN 9781989496077 (softcover)
Classification: LCC PS8623.I524 D68 2020 | DDC C811/.6—dc23

For Eli

There is no turning back to be someone I might have been. Now there will only ever be multiples of me.
  – Mary Jo Bang, "Self-Portrait in the Bathroom Mirror"

All "portraits" are also self-portraits.
  – Lynne Tillman, *Men and Apparitions*

Contents

Contents

Tinnitus

In Italy volumes have been composed on how light
fulfills a room, volumes so deafening ringing replaces

silence for days after. Or not ringing as much as
a buzzing hum – an elastic holding wax paper

over the loo tube. O kazoo, no one truly loves you.
Too much oomph to your oompah, too many

disclaimers before the performance. Share precious
memories more, that's what the earthlings do

when being honest with their emotions, when
screaming at the sound guy who came to lay out cable

and leave early. All the same problems plague these people,
these people of the contaminated memory.

These people of a terra nova nowhere close
to the mainland values too loud for the old and un-

earplugged, who can't expect to be in the same light-
filled room without acquiring an ache, arthritis

of the ears. Earlier in this poem I wrote, "light fulfills
a room." Allow me to elaborate: light fulfills

a room like love promises to fulfill a lonely kazoo's
longing; like breath fulfills the lungs of a woodwind

by adding an individual's air that runs the circuit,
or like assumption fulfills memory by contaminating

what fulfills the blank spaces – eyes demanding worth
in missing letters, erasures, censored text, bars

blacking out names. It was the ever-poetic cicadas
that swapped the *e* for an *a* and moved the mouth harp

from Jew to jaw, keeping the electric twang but dropping
any accusation of Nazism that may come their way

when awakening to a new world after seventeen years
underground with only nymphs to form opinions with.

Crickets as critics of sunsets: the first to correctly
detect the effect of air pollution, the dye of the sky

that was assumed to be natural. Natural like the beginning
of this poem felt. But so much has happened since beginning.

And the light. I forgot about the light. Did I illustrate how
it "fulfills a room"? How rooms defer completion without

this essence? Perhaps I should have quoted from the "volumes."
And the rhyming was inconsistent. And though I cannot remember

how or why, I took the concept for this poem from "Italy,"
the title poem of Donald Britton's only collection, in which

he writes, "I'm still confused about why I mentioned Italy
At the beginning of this poem, especially since

It's all a terrible lie."

Failed Questions

Survivors

It would be lying to say that this cold reading will
age well, or that this musician knows how to play
his zither, but the performance sounds convincing

so don't stop the trot and canter for an affluent few
while their donations spiral into the wishing well,
draining away like the last of the rainwater almond

farmers prayed for. The droughts caused by breeding
out arsenic from the most widespread milk substitute,
scoffing at the modern crop. Topiary cities reverse-

engineered from English gardens to public housing
would have been of better use than defending golf
courses from encroaching deserts. Two conclusions

are clear: either Los Angeles will return to powder
or be dragged under the ocean. Time to run through
the survival scenarios again. Time to start dressing

as peasants again. It's suspect to trust any type of
identification that isn't self-applied, so forgive the
snickering, it's just hard to take this seriously after

anxious nights pouring over ornate impossibilities
for a physically alive architecture – floral umbilicals
tethering the Earth to organic space stations; shoots

producing their own oxygen; self-repairing elevators
for the survivors to ascend – and it would still be lying
to declare it a solution. Best-case scenario is the shitty

wizard conjures drizzle and the director remembers
his name. All are imposters and no one knows anyone
anymore in these days of botched botany. These days

of meticulously constructed personas, questionnaires
for gathering information on vegetation some feel deep,
spiritual empathy with. Or at least what is considered

spiritual when the messiahs are self-proclaimed and the
survivors, decoding some scraps they were able to save,
seeking meaning in endings, are strangers to each other.

Harmony

Nine times out of ten the most alien organism
humans can imagine is still humanoid
in appearance, still wants to talk and the thing

about taking back what was said is that
it's an impossible contract two parties
agree to understanding it all depends on their

mutual will to perform forgetful. Near perfect
but born wounded, lacking technical know-how.
Runts without a grammar needed to know why

these semi-images collage hodgepodge. Exists
as affirmation. Good dog, you've done your best.
Tonight you shall sleep in the big bed. But once

more you must recite the story, and this time
without the prompts provided by the interrogator,
who is impatiently waiting to go home to his

small family. A cousin to take care of, a cat
to let in. Not everyone has someone who waits
for them. A collision reconstruction unit drops

absorbent dust to seep up leftover liquid
from the car that crashed into the bridge
that bridges the dip in the road that flooded

in the winter storm. An agreement between
adults who fail to remember December's push,
push, push – to what? The right to not be alone.

A contract between car and bridge, dust and liquid.
Memory and reality: a moulding done in crumbling
Play-Doh; a stunned ring from a dumbbell left on

the far side of a Lazy Susan no one uses because
it was never intended to be lived in as an asylum,
only a place to put our mutually unthinkable things.

The Revelry of Others

> The revelry of others showed up as
> bags under my eyes.
> — Ange Mlinko, "Dentro de la Tormenta"

Driven by Brandon through Buffalo and the Poconos
to snowy Greenpoint to meet Vito and Lise and look

for old eccentric records at some skeletal weirdo's,
I find myself enduring proximity like a dull twinge

not worthy of ibuprofen. At the military café, a shirtless
man on TV is euphoric on football. After lunch I'm aghast

in ineffable, unfuckwithable, newfangled new-found lands
I indulged in a way that is by definition of interest to me:

unease. Homesickness, I lit you on fire just to smack it out
and unnecessarily beat myself up in the process. But once

I succumbed, numbing myself by gifted food and drink,
I embarked on noticing all the small moving parts often

overlooked, all the atmospheric outspokenness around.
I didn't know it could snow in another city, but I learned.

Suddenly ski masks seemed sensible instead of lecherous,
some seasonal local norm. Travelling in twos interrupted

my reading. Travelling (not far) intensified night on the air
mattress and itched my nerves the next evening at dinner

with so many unfamiliar voices challenging each other for
airspace. Vito and Lise, how do they do it? Hosting, talking –

talking, hosting. I will forget to send them a Christmas card
and build a gilded guilt of it. The worst the introvert heard

was an invite's *bing-bing*ing, the doorbell's *ding-dong*ing
as I sigh against the windowpane, readying for the storm.

The Narcissism of Sleep

A few feet from where I feign sleep water explores
a lazy maze only contractors can map, obscured

by what have come to be called *walls*, spelled
by semi-sameness: a practice not taught but

handed down witness to witness in an open
secret culture war whose rules are recorded

in pantomime, an unfashionable proto-clown
in the metaphysical tradition of self-reflection

and lying awake, listening to the house sounds
that make themselves known only to insomniacs,

those who acknowledge the anonymous water,
the meme-like routine, the itchy superstructure

wandering an opaque array, fatiguing a bad dad
joke's welcome by worrying its threadbare punch-

line at a sleep disorder support group where I learned
about Scooter – his podcast you don't need to listen to

in order to undergo its lull, its homemaking
of unthinking non-silence that halts it all –

tolerating enough time for the weight to lift
cynicism from the narcissism of sincere sleep.

*Ooooo*s and *Woooo*s

Where the protruding barn nail tore
my elderly feather-hemorrhaging coat,
a hundred thousand threads were born
again and aroused the windows, trembling
not from the nervousness of meeting us but
the choppy-lake gusts, water guts guffawing
at winter storm hilarities, which were, to be
fair, pretty funny but in a way we would never
laugh at in front of our owners, unlike electric
heaters' exposed orange coils, begging to be
diddled and you grew irritable from snatching
my hand by the wrist and no one slept with all
the wind's asthmatic choir frisking the exterior,
patting down the heritage cottage nonchalantly,
the casual touching suggesting it knew nothing
was hidden inside, confidence I wish we shared
when the *ooooo*s and *woooo*s grew in intensity
as afternoon lurched along like ice slowly exploding
from glaciers or the lake's glass eczema whispering
as it meets itself all over again and again and again.

Two Kinds of Ice

Almost awake enough
in the place where we
were wanted but not
welcomed, ice ships
creep an island made
of bays, perspiring
after a three year float
from Greenland. Tylenol
towering above the boat
we paid Bruce $200
to tour us in, the derelict
fishing villages his parents
were born in and the one
built for the miniseries
left to rot. *If there is
anything you need ask,
ask.* A button summons
the flight attendant who
has a serious smile while
warning about moose.
They run this season,
killing several drivers
every year as their slim
bulk collapses through wind-
shields. Ghost in the mean-
spirited rental. Our host
said not to enter the attic
or remove the burlap
from the original owner's

portrait. So we didn't,
and are alive because of it,
free to hike the lichen trails,
trees swaying like Medusa
snakes, seducing us closer
to the ground cover, down
on hands and knees, ears
pressed to the clicking
symphony of tiny life
tolerating our weight.

Failed Interview Questions

How loud was it in utero
in the midst of an insides'
white noise roaring away
like a river or the engine
that powers a cicada's
whirring purr as it sheds
an exoskeleton it wore
as some wear expressions
comfortably year in, year
out until a sketch artist
depicts it and upon seeing
a hyperbole of their face,
rids it from their repertoire.

Is the silence you hear now
that the drone of mom's body
keeping you alive is gone
the reason why you cry with
such gusto and confidence
in the electric mechanism
that makes the bees' buzz
recognizable, comfortable
to those of us who grew
up unallergic and knowing
that the colonies the keepers
spoke of were hives vibrating
with visible static electricity.

Do you realize how useless
I am to you, that I cannot keep
you alive alone, I am a need
as much as you but you are
narcissism without centre
and I am anxiety measured
by the way I judge my double
self-portrait and don't think
that means you, look-alikes
live in the internal, that artificial
visual of you that existed before
you existed, mind-made bait
designed to lure me to you.

Who are you reaching for
when you suddenly wake,
arms outstretched and panic
in your eyes, startled to still
be here and then immediately
lose consciousness, baffling
the hushed tones we speak
as you dreamfeed in near-dark
with busy fingers improvising
on an instrument only you can
play, self-soothing to a melody
only you can hear, learning
to dream by Braille.

Are your murmuring coos
responses to my attempts
at conversation with you;
something unknowable
only for me, unintentional
code whose meaning lives
in my tries at translation,

my fidgeting with a cipher
you squirm on the playmat,
or are you playing at how
to enjoy a fussy tête-à-tête,
an auto-interview, intimacy
that must fail to be near real.

Why can't I complete
a question for you
and is it unfair to ask
anything of you even
if what I want is a face
I can believe was made
for me and not because
you are discovering
internal movement,
engines and electric
mechanisms grinding
against your brain and
inspiring contortions

I interpret as a dance
depicting the frustration
of experience when time
is only the present, memory
something yet to be learned
then overlooked, but that is
impossible for me, my lack
of hormones is a split link;
makes me a citizen-tourist
in an aimless authoritarian
country whose rules I abide
adoringly, for I chose to live
like this: in love with my tiny

benevolent sovereign
awakening to his reign.

Lying to Children about Santa

There's nothing wrong with trying
to assemble lists, but on our honey-
moon in Spain we skipped the spot
where Lorca was shot. Lacan loved
Justine, his dog, because he thought
she only saw him for him. The man
I called grandfather used to sing me
"Goodnight, Irene" as I tried to sleep,
"Wild Blue Yonder" when we went up
escalators. What was he trying to do?
What's the "do"? Tormentor thinks
himself a worldbuilder, puts paper
over the windows to signal change
to the neighbours but soon the core
will price him out. O maintenance
O maintenance, look at your lights
flash! So much emergency for what?
Not this gash, I hope. All war wounds
are bragging mouths left open, agape
at being once again owned by urchin
young enough not to know you can't
remember being born because never
has there ever been a moment when
outside space and celibacy wasn't
something intended of children.

Lying as Wishful Thinking

The year of reading about Freud
being an endearing fuck-up. The year
of innermost list building, list looking.

The year of friends falling and the year
of learning to walk in the snow so also
the year of really seeing your feet move

for the first time. Your feet and nothing
else making a muffled crunch as they
drop away. The year of admitting money

might have played a part; of reading
that Freud was in love with his drug
dealer. But where did you read that

and how could anyone know such
a thing? The last year of the penny
and the year before a new PIN

for each card. The year of lying
as wishful thinking, of willing
the indignity down and watching

it bob back up, no matter how much
worthless copper put in its pockets.
The year of more disastrous magic

and Freud inventing narcissism
as a diagnosis for clients resistant
to analysis. The lost year. The year

of augmentation and of associating
olive oil with bananas. The last year
of olive oil and bananas; of carelessly

constructing the memory of olive oil
and bananas – of unlived lives lived
alongside an arbitrary month amount

that drags at each end. Sluggish fantasies,
erotic or not: drowning swimmers flailing
their arms to grasp their rescuer, dragging

the lifeguard down with them. The year of
redefining infection: germs as pessimism,
the unconscious things said that are only

audible when the audio is reversed.
The year of living fundamentally,
the old believers returning to Siberia

only to be discovered by geologists
forty years later and die of exposure
to diseases they had no immunity to,

diseases they fled but were found by.
The year of falling out of love with Freud
and the year of summoning the strength

to tell him to find his coke elsewhere now;
of Freud, wandering from chemist to chemist,
really seeing his feet move for the first time.

A Home Can't Be Abandoned if It Was Never Lived In

> The idea that memories are stored in *individual neurons* is
> preposterous: how and where is the memory stored in the cell?
> – Robert Epstein, "The Empty Brain"

A psychologist is expressing frustration
surrounding the likening of computers
to the human brain: chain-link versus
innumerable esophaguses perforating
sea sponges abducted from the sea floor.

A psychologist, Robert Epstein, is frustrated
with sticky, poetry-making metaphors of
hydraulic automata and information storage
we use in lieu of understanding voids, fearing
the semi-permanence of occurrence, fearing

path-fashioning burrowers unendingly
rerouting ekphrastic warrens recounting
the cursive of rustling leaves. Currents drifting
like kelp loosened from its forest. Currents
like late autumn air soliciting us with familiar

wisps suggestive of, yes, death, but also how
it feels to afford an afternoon of boredom,
an affluent restlessness, suspended anticipation
desiring desire. The lone child caged on a plain
of tall, dry August grass, whose anxiety finally

concedes when an adult parts the curtains
of the biggest window they were forbidden
to approach. A former friend I no longer
speak to once told me that the body craves
what it's allergic to; consumption is a duty

to DNA, the slow drip of heredity hierarchy
we assume is natural because we have read
about it somewhere. False memories of early
pleasure built from whatever pornography
washes upon us daily. Not the hard drive's

recall, the mind's recognition: recognizable
mesmerizations of two kinds of fear: the gun
and unknowable rational behind the gun;
the blade and biopsy results you claim not to
have heard, though your eyes say otherwise.

Between Wars

Between the wars I found myself glowing
from four pale ales under an unforeign sun.

This ceasefire became real worry that was
embodied by the uncoded day-residue few

found time to laugh at. Sarcasm's shitty shield
that depicts hand-wringing as the first flails

of an infant as his mother sinks him into
the chlorinated water of the community

pool. Madeleine of bleach. An involuntary
glance at what loiters in peripheral. A sun,

unforeign and uncoded, emphasizing
how right I am to worry about relaxing.

Thank you, sun. Let me take this moment
to say I understand why you burn, why

you mark me in war zones of melanoma.
But I draw the line at your interpretations

of these pigment splatters. Neither of us
has been to war, yet you are so sure this

is an in-between; that these blottings are trying
to paint a statement. "Look at that huge ground

arrow," said the pilot. "Why didn't they see me?"
asked the survivor, arms outstretched, ready

to be run through by his own point. A wolf
worries an ungulate's neck and this is a bad

joke that took too long to get to the point.
But here, between wars, there is time, sun.

Time to collect as many stones as it takes
to make a sign explaining who to rescue.

Travel and Leisure

There are many poems about bees
failing to be bees in the liberal world
because of new chemicals and sound,
because of displacement and disquiet,
because of office windows and karma
and how sex concepts have unfastened,
and because bees represent failure,
the failure to protect the dependent
and light-sensitive from the light
they never even recognized as light
until it was embarrassed upon them –
but not this poem. This is an earnest
truther's two minute mini-warning
dolled up as awkward art, a caution sign:
look: here I stand, swarmed and stung
by the little bastards. Don't listen to me,
of course everyone is still middle-class,
what else would we be? Know the grass
is so proudly green because it was fertilized
by a winter's worth of dog shit and as long
as you understand the plight is not yours
forever, you may have it for now. Remember
that those who still depend on phone booths
know they don't deserve gifts, they deserve
to work hard and to pay for things. If not us,
then who is rightly entitled to brunch
on the burial grounds of their economic
ancestors? Come, this traveller's anxiety
isn't doing the tour group any favours.

Let go of the local visible world and join
this vacation that can be paid for later
with assumed salaries you'd be stupid
not to accrue. All the years put in to it –
collecting stinging insects so children
will have something to write poems about –
of course you should demand it all back,
or force the facility to face the implication
that we are who we are because of a flaw
in the framework; a famous missed stitch
in the fibre optic thread physicists call string
theory, which may or may not have anything
to do with divinity, closer to a tiny typo in
the manuscript that made its way to press
and is what it is because of its permanence.

Repro Ditto

after Bees

Doubles are reproductions that realize
enough's enough and knock it off,
recognizing the mechanics of a ménage
à trois wishing for one echo, not an array

of bodies arranged in a particular way.
Meticulous lists lined up, year after year,
waiting for a knowing nod. Full of new
music, but just because there is music

doesn't mean music has to be always on.
Personally, I liked it more before I read it
again and the tower looked taller from far
away. The sound of thousands of lifelong

fans sighing, lowering their faces, rubbing
their screen-sore eyes, colonizing a culture
cube our Internet ignored, dominating it
in squatters' manoeuvres. *Nostalgia*: Greek

compound consisting of *homecoming*
and *ache* or *pain*. Reaching back to
the *ache* or *pain* as double. Memory
as knock-off and knock-off as Boris Karloff

makeup. Ménage à trois, meaning *house-
hold of three*, or, the first reproduction's
like-minded hangry frenemy. "Doubles are
reproductions that realize enough's enough

and knock it off." That is a terrible lie.
The reproduction only wishes it could choose
to reproduce. No, not sibling rivalry; Oedipal
aggression. Cog as clog as saboteur. Cancer

cells curing cancer cells. Frenemy because
of need and hangry because of resource
guarding. Gardens ravaged by look-alikes.
Repetitious representations chanting,

chanting in dog Latin a mostly imitation
meat meant to remind the eater of texture
and taste. How gauche the barely affordable
one-bedroom reclaiming crumbling brick

back from authenticity. An old city acts out
for attention, but with no parent to appease,
who's there to say, "*Shhh, shhh.* Shut up"?
Is an only child an unlucky child? Is music

on at the moment? What is that buzzing
hum and when did the bees come back?
They envy the cicadas' "poetic significance."
(Dear Reader, I'm not quoting; I'm caging

ideas in ditto marks so poetry isn't mistaken
for fact.) "Bees." Please. Best to just come out
and admit it, you were faking near extinction.
Sitting in your cell, sombre. Sober. Dear Reader,

may I be honest with you? I am reaching back.
I lost part of the first draft of "Repro Ditto,"
the poem you are now reading, so I'm rewriting
it from memory. A *homecoming* of *ache* or

pain. A "household of three": me, the first,
lost draft, and the one you are reading now,
nostalgic as it is. I remember originally one
bee specifically – let's call him Doppelgänger.

I remember mentioning a monarch –
let's call her Yayoi Kusama – dominated
by trypophobia, an aversion to the sight
of irregular patterns or clusters of small holes

or bumps and in a book by Donald Winnicott
I remember reading, "The fear of domination
does not lead groups of people to avoid being dominated;
on the contrary, it draws them towards a specific

or chosen domination." I remember black/yellow
beads between infinity mirrors that dubbed them.
Each image a fib, a savvy divvy of reverberation,
an excuse deployed to avoid the self-righteous

original and the ostriching of authenticity cultists
who are only now learning what a face looks like.
They burned Gutenberg's stupid machine,
they smashed jars of royal jelly to preserve

the memory of their one true queen, her beads,
the perfectly cracked shards of infinity mirrors
fused back into an strained Pangaea, a second
faultless Earth inside our own. A second Earth

that knows it came first and pities mimics
walking surface-side in a gullible glimmer,
oblivious to birthing order, pleading adoption
as a defence, propaganda applied by principal

ancestors who were trying to do what a queen
would want: multiply by making masks siblings,
stabbing eyeholes into a portrait and sporting it
around while demanding answers. I remember

unabashedly playing with plagiarism, calling it
appropriation to make myself sound intelligent.
So of course I remember Joe Brainard and also
I remember wanting to convey envy. I remember

demanding answers from the colony, grafted
branches, wisdom of the unoriginal and yet
I'm still confused about why I mentioned bees
in the title of this poem since it's all a terrible lie.

Decorative Knots

Decorative Knots

Amniotic Oceanic

1.

It's like this that children resent their parents:
wonky and handmade, repetitious yet special,

a unique kink interpreted as nausea when watching
tadpoles squirm – squirming instead of swimming

because they cannot be called frogs yet; not even
sperm per se, only little larva who benefit from

the soft confrontation of another ecosystem's song
that in darkness releases pent-up heat from stone,

cement and concrete walls, ripening urban orchards
that feed few but rely on many shadows for nightwork.

2.

When moving through the heat the heat realizes
physically into feral imagery vocabulary that tries

but fails to envision the entire city, throbbing
with sauna rocks' stockpiled radiation, forced

to acknowledge not choosing a side is still a form
of side choosing between two ponds, neither of

which want more members, but when asked will say,
"Of course we need and want; what, other than water,

is there to hold in these wonky, handmade mugs
we only use to spare their makers' emotions?"

3.

It's grotesque to gaze into a bisected fig because
it succeeds in signifying an idea of the internal

with all its mysterious wet bits as seen in a doc
about how frogs and flies give birth – offspring

spilling from their host's split skin like sweat seeps
from skin, staining black garments with a salty frost

that labels its wearer as one who does not consider
the temperature, has time to seek out the cool side

of the pullout even if the cool side of the pullout
is cool because a shadow sleeps there nowadays.

4.

The dog suns herself until she can't take it anymore
then flops into the patio's shadow, caught between

the need for heat and the want of comfort; the need
to breed and the fear of being split open by miniature

scaremongers raring to stand up on their own spindly
shanks and proclaim, "If I could draw I would draw

a comfort made out of a wet red hug whose household
sound is an oceanic echo hushed by an amniotic ocean

everyone spends a brief pre-birth breathing then a long
life realizing that non-aquatic animals must live on land."

The Self-Interviewing River

I didn't want to call this poem
"The Self-Interviewing River,"
after a line by Fred Wah and
after the flux of running water
and all portraits as self-portraits,
but then I kept hearing about
this nostalgia tent pole, tenet
of conservatism, and *ontogeny*
was a word I saw written and read
twice in one afternoon, some neat
spume easily disregarded as froth
to be skimmed by at least two
people I know, one who I pay
and one who advised not to
avoid and that in this family
when we have to cry, we cry
out pleading to please ignore
or find it in you to pretend,
please try or else aggravate
because it's already August,
and you barely left the city,
let alone attempted a pass
at something like an apology.

Decorative Knots

Plainspoken decorative knots,
painstakingly tied glass tubes,
undenominational insofar as
it's not worth distinguishing
individuals from the overall
effect, but important enough
to stand back, let the stressed
eyes relax, depth perception
blur permanently, become one
unconcerned by sight, plucky
enough to feel out the passage
by guy wire, counting twists
as the alley narrows and allies
fall behind, then the likeness
will step forward, drop robe,
give a little twirl, begging for
honest opinions; honest opinions
unfiltered by social niceties or
personal curation: a selection of
sub-organisms mounted on white
board and organized by colour,
shape and texture so those who
can't stomach seeing a dead thing
can still tell what they're touching.

Hissing of Summer Lawns

Wheat fields in the wind
pulsing with air welling
up inside a glittering of
green on summerland
grassland, the hissing
of August lawns as air
snakes out of blades
like auto lot inflatables,
one-legged air-dancers
for a yawning audience,
gazillions vying for envy,
swing stirring up sway
in tinsel tassel anemones,
an aquatic shimmering
of chartreuse piano keys
twinkling across pastures,
meadow combs pleasured
by submitting to a barber
out of love with reflection,
the melancholy of offering
six hours for consideration,
how outside sees you, a face
and glass in osmosis, the day
like dolphins during coitus,
up for anything in an ocean,
a gleaming saline ray ocean,
a mercury ripple plain ocean,
that was turned against them.

Summerland

Being teetotal didn't stop the front lawn from drowning
as dramatically as possible in plain sight of the evening
porch-sitters, gingerly sipping highballs while the post-
solstice sun set on a Skype session with gramps. Go tilt

another one back in recognition of the responsibility all
Scientologists acknowledge. For though they would love
to romp and play in the open air, they have info to unveil.
Volunteerism: antitoxin to privilege's nonlethal venom

cramps. The whitest mime's temper tantrum. Validation
of taste, a little hipper, happier paying more for ethically
made electronic music. Wasn't it the shut-in who yelled,
"At the Festival I was surprised to find the Cathedral still

incomplete! The Church must have Photoshopped out
the cranes one can see from all over the City!" In a jiffy
the old kerfuffle forgets past damage of summer storms,
reversing sewer water into mud rooms of slutty grooms.

It was the same creeping speak that grew hydroponically
and hidden by fathers from their children, who, ironically,
made due with hand-me-down maracas gifted from jilted
glee club coaches preaching parataxis. Separatists will

want – no – need to make the active connections in an art
piece of white, pixelated clouds, instantly recognizable
from the famous video game; the isolated upper half
lackadaisically scrolling by while viewers do little in life.

The Gap

Though I cannot be sure, I believe
there to be a body of water beyond
this wide cluster of trees. Something
in the air and a moment ago I swear
I saw what could have been a seabird.
Something in the mouth and esophagus.
What did the poet call it? Ah, a lozenge.
A nervous-green cough candy gliding
like an osprey, inauspicious to the fish
in its throat. But back at the tourist
trap no one is wondering where I
wandered off to. So no one is here
to remind me a mirage is a misquote
I forgot to correct. A mirage is a mistake
in the senses, senselessness as seen
from the assured clearing, the gap
in the green to authenticate the lake or
whatever is wet, wavy and obscured by
this fir fence. An allegory is a long way
to walk around to avoid confronting
an alleged original, an accoutrement
remembrance put on first impression,
a spurious condiment, a defeatist's
definition of nostalgia. *Make it great
again*, says a tedious weirdo adrift
in the woods and too stubborn
to admit they weren't here first.

White Christmas Tree

The great thing about your kind
is kindness; collapsible glowing
honest non-needles inhabiting
a cardboard box, an egg's interior
eager, flamboyant and born phony
the great thing about you is that you
never try to be anything you're not, no
you hum melancholy holiday melodies
that could Xerox yuletide year-round
potentially cranking out so much fake
green, tarted-up pines and firs blush
and the great thing about you
is that you will never know
how slowly you're disappearing
one wilting icicle at a time, snowing
tinfoil and the great thing about you
is how naturally we will forget you.

Quotes

Who said that authenticity is the idea
that originality has inherent value

that cannot be outspent and its replicas
are reluctant to kill each other? Not the

sitcom's drop-in neighbour, not the hum
you're hearing. It's a haunting, a homage

to and snuffing out of something worth
worshipping. Try not to hate your father

figure for dragging you to the shooting
range that rang for years after. Still rings,

"We're all just trying our best." A nice
thing to say to yourself when the noise

returns to reckon. What colour were the
participation ribbons in your grade school?

The ones they gave out to us unathletic on
track and field day. Mine were aquamarine

and for too long I thought it was a thing
I shouldn't be ashamed of. Beginning this

book is a poem called "Tinnitus" (and ending
it is a poem called "Double Self-Portrait"),

in which I write, "ringing replaces silence
for days after." After what? "The Volumes,"

I write and then I try and fail to define it for
you. And right now, as I write this new poem,

"Repro Ditto," I'm trying to decide if it's worth
attempting once again to illustrate for you

how silence is darkness of sound and impossible
as bodies emit as much illumination as they do

reverberation. Is it even possible to show you
that when I say, "Volumes have been composed

on how light fulfills a room, volumes so deafening
ringing replaces silence for days after. Or not

ringing as much as a buzzing hum," I'm trying
to do something unoriginal in an original way

and that when I wrote about participation
ribbons and being unathletic, I meant poetry.

Whenever I'm obtuse, know I mean poetry
as echoing memory – each repetition a fib,

a dub weakening in volume and clarity
the farther it travels with you as fact,

especially since it's all a terrible lie.

Ekphrasis! Ekphrasis!

Double Self-Portrait

after Jeff Wall

I wanted to make a picture coming out
of a literary source in the idea

of the double in which the identity
of the character was maybe not

concludable, so I tucked my grey
sweatshirt into my belted blue

jeans to better match my look-alike.
He wore wine-dark corduroys

that complement our couch. "Red,"
I said when I first saw it. "It's red."

"More mauve than cherry," said
my blushing double, arms crossed

and hesitant to invite you to sit in
the white wire chair you referred to

as a flipped arachnid dead in its web,
backlit by heatstroke and twin domestic.

It's safe to assume that one of us sired
the other, grafted himself to the sofa

corner where a pink blanket peeled
back; cracked the door and took a nap

in practical cibachrome Vancouver,
awakening later that afternoon

as brother-fathers to one another,
both in incest and attendance.

How Does It Feel

after Bridget Moser

There's a filter on the window,
meant to protect us from the harsh

afternoon sunlight. But all it seems
to do is make the room unnecessarily

blue as you merge with the furniture,
the white lamp and aqua sofa, in ways

the Swedes never intended. Trapped
behind the vista veil, handless sleeves

flap like a drowning thing's flippers.
I don't understand your massive sweater.

You swim in its cobalt while the cold glow
of the light box and its rotating ski scene

illuminates your contemplative face.
You chew a pen but take no notes on

that murky in-betweenness, the timbre
of dreams fading as blonde hair turtles

into a high woollen neckline as you
emerge from under plush bedding

that belongs to a hotel room you paid for,
therefore, entitled to explore as you see fit.

So make an aqueduct of your body to bridge
the chairs and when you find the costume

jewellery, concealed within a hardcover,
pause for a minute to pose with it, breathing.

The Playthrough

In the time it takes my avatar to cross the viaduct,
a pack of programmers hastily conceives the far

side where optics are unbelievable. A resin coat
the world wears. Too clear crystalline water crashes

the game again and again. The desktop's fan fails,
sending real life heat and a worrying whirring

from the short tower. Lubricate those eyes
so the viewers won't see how bloodshot six hours

of gaming makes them. And remember to tell them
not to forget to subscribe. And remember the corridor

is an illusion of perspective and light. Put down the
energy drink, your hands are shaking. Spoiler alert,

this hot-cum-cool medium makes for a satisfying
watch and the invisible wall can be glitched through

by riding a trash can like the promised sky rocket
of the upper level that is only accessible by mind

games, intricate fuckery that is meant to fit fun
into the part of the day that makes it regrettable. A failed

twenty-four hour mechanics that constructs sunrises
out of flashlights found in hidden cabinets. What has

become of the day? Where did the light go? It can't
be all about the kill team. None of this effort matters

if there's no record of us screaming at one another.

The Playthrough

The time it takes me to walk from Queen to King
IRL is the time it takes a chatty gamer to design

a convincing expression of surprise. A gullible glimmer
of plastic ponchos on sexless torsos strolling around

like awkward androids taking first steps. Pixelated
limbs ominously oscillating their glitchy shadows

across flat confetti grass. Get ready to re-up lives
for the obedient employment of acknowledging

the company that provides the software, the hardware
and the game itself. A daylight seance is a kind of trick

and a category of magic. Snap out of it, it can't be
all instant ramen all the time. I don't own the right

type of system to fool around here, so I voyeur down
the immaculately conceived hallway in the compound

cultists constructed out of leftover digital debris,
made to, if you know how to do it, just, like, *be*

your quintessential self, *man*. Me? I need to squeeze
into a clean line of sight through the kind of person

valiant enough to make a lifestyle out of it. My god,
what happened to you? What has become of flashlight

mechanics? An obvious relation in the rise of memoir
and the popularity of POV perspective as seen watching

an unknowable nerd chat while playing computer games.

Sunrise with Sea Monsters

after JMW Turner

Was the face intentional, or were you practising flexing
your pure medium of middle light? *The obscure pink swirl
probably depicts fish,* speculates the Tate. A sign of scurvy
in a seaside town waiting for the end. In 1906 the National
Gallery gave the incomplete work title and focus. Corporeal
consequence for an optical illusion, atmospheric conditions,
a golden Om interpreted as water because you adored water,
and later, whalers. England was obsessed with sea monsters,
and you were treating a toothache with acetate of morphia,
reconnecting the shrapnel of leftover delirium into a Pangaea,
momentarily abstracting romanticism to expose a flattened
amber ambience; a frog face hanging in a honeyed diamond.

And Then We Saw the Daughter of the Minotaur

after Leonora Carrington

who had intentionally lived in the maze to practise flexing
under her red robe. *Her habit of refusal of the world she was
born into began early*, Kathryn Davis writes in her intro to your
complete stories. 1953, a room waiting for the end, led by your
friend, the pope of the plant-men and his corporeally robed kids.
Atmospheric consequences on the ceiling are optical conditions
for the orbs on the table. The Spanish obsessed with surrealism
and you adored horses and an uncanny category of gastronomy
somewhere between a stomach ache and speculative astronomy
attempting to reconnect shrapnel from another Earth abandoned
by romantics afraid of abstraction; illuminating a dancing mural
that silky dogs lying in debris barely have time to acknowledge.

An Oral History of
Homesick Music

No child ever recovers from not having cured his parents.
– Adam Phillips, "On Not Getting It," *Missing Out*

Let's not lament the death
of music made with guitars.

Death as in Alzheimer's
is the cure for memory

and we fear not remembering.
Not remembering the address

of your childhood house. Home,
the house you called home,

still there and calm without you.
They cut down the tree you

planted with family. The tree
you had forgotten about. Rock

gardens can fend for themselves
and albums, phono and photo,

are organized to get forgotten
in a box in the back of a closet.

An Oral History of
Dad-Rap

We'd back away from this tedious weirdo, that is, for the same
reasons [Adam] Phillips backs away, in his writing, from any
kind of essentialism.
     – Mark O'Connell, review of *Unforbidden Pleasures*,
       by Adam Phillips, *New York Times*

The need to know what happened
before the explanation refreshed

the rat's nest of reactions, a braid
that coupled some twitchy clock-

work to the habitual bridge-burner's
livestream of the sex doll's unboxing:

all this and more stored on a USB key
hidden in a marital bed's bedpost

and hoarded in a storage locker. It sits
waiting, trying to look nonchalant

in rented darkness, confident yet twin
to lamentation. Explanation always

travels down and what is passed on
often breaks apart upon re-entry

in an atmosphere of a second Earth
that idiots insisted never existed.

Werewolf and Birdman

after David Altmejd

Show how you constructed your sister's face out of a dazzling cavity.
Show how gently the melting men made of grasping hands performed
a sixty-nine. Show how to execute the patented technique you invented

to precisely crack mirrors, mending shatters into reflective web. Decay
as labour, mould fuzz as fur. Show how to crystallize werewolves' grey
matter until shards pierce skull. Show how hollow the birdman can be,

how hollow the plastic apparatus was before filled with clay decapitations
in Tetris, the buffoon's manhood, masculinity as something to be smeared
like thick liquid, pink, green and aqua. Pineapples, aghast at their new lips

and jealous of the cherub hair in an erupting lattice, a gush of Spanish
moss tossed from a geode chunk. Orgy society suspended in a clear grid
erected as a souvenir from the spectacle. Orally organic like all orifices

opening upon fleshy tissue, O-faced stucco cave mouths in sudden
recognition of flesh folding into flesh. *During sex beauty is sure of
itself. During sex the body is alone* as all bodies are alone, together.

Cranberry Bog

after Yayoi Kusama

Show how impossible it is to start without acknowledging your dot
obsession. Polkas self-obliterating, perforating pumpkins, arachnid
eyes multiplied: your patented technique. Infinity mirrors, a reflective

red web run through by white bees fleeing Manhattan in ailing health
to Japan to write *shockingly visceral and surrealistic novels, short stories
and poetry.* A grand orgy to awaken the dead, a narcissus garden of orbs

in a pajama-themed stanza, an anemone caresses a happening of naked
bodies queued up for your paint. Cover them in a pox of dots contracted
through skin-on-skin contact: thick kisses: pink, yellow, blue, but black

in the photographs from the time before the discovery of colour. Lungfish
learning to skip from a sea and breathe surface air. An eruption of roseola
the school mimics en masse. Vox pop spots, concentric specks hollering hoi

polloi from orgasmic maws scattershot across gallery walls. A dizzying
of portholes, portals to more portholes on a Seuss-beast's back. A beast
whose beauty is sure as bubbles huddle are beautiful and sure, together.

Sex Club

No one came to here to hear me read
poetry. They came, then felt almost no
disgrace. I came to gawk at the art
on the walls. I came to talk about a Goya,

housed in the Museo del Prado,
Madrid, depicting his muse,
María Cayetana de Silva, 13th Duchess of Alba,
scaring the shit out of her servant,

who defends herself with a crucifix.
The label text describes the duchess
as "whimsical." The awkward moment
when getting naked in front of people

comes with not knowing if the peeling
sunburn on your back has fully healed.
The focus of the painting is the duchess's
black cascade of hair from the back

as she grasps her dueña by the collar. The terror
on the old woman's face: now *that's* comedy.
To enter you must be a member. A possibility
that you might see someone you work with,

or, worse, are related to. Though never
confirmed, it's rumoured that the two were
lovers due to certain innuendo. "No means no"
is rule number one. After her husband died,

Goya moved in with the duchess and painted
her portrait regularly. "No sex in the pool"
is number two. Some nudes. The membership
doubles as a waiver agreeing not to be offended

by screwing or nudity. Artists and aristocracy
are often collaborators, but still I wonder
why I came here by myself when half the club
is strictly "couples only." Of all moments

to immortalize they picked that cruel prank
and there's no use in poetry if no one listens
to me feeling nothing while watching orgies.
I laughed so loudly that a docent *shhh*ed me.

Gender of Connectors
and Fasteners

No one in particular asked me to pardon
poetry's preoccupation with power
ballads and baseball. But for you I will.
For you I will stop ceaselessly humming

the music my co-workers whistle all shift –
a reluctant soundtrack to sleeplessness
and the restless art on the walls, winking
at us on our way to bed, trying to get a gasp.

What a whimsical haunt. What an awkward
moment, undressing in front of fake paintings
that hide the eyeholes of the crawl space.
What will they make of the Plath tattoos

we got in Boston? All of *Ariel* cascading
in black ink down our backs. They'll focus
on the peeling scabs not yet fully healed
instead of, as we would hope, the terror

of living in a building where every room
is watched by a member of the crawl space.
Hush-hush hallways used to catch the comedy,
the previously mentioned gasps of someone

you work with, or, better yet, are related to
on their way to bed. For you I will ignore any
innuendo spilling from lovers or husbands.
One of us has to die first. The duchess,

the painting of the duchess, has whispered
to me that it is you. Though never confirmed,
it is rumoured that Goya was her lover. Husband

and pool boy, artist and gigolo, double deadened

and nude; screwing aristocrats when collaborating,
attempting earnest collaborating with the culture
club. Of all moments to admit the truth – at least
what is considered the truth after the cruel prank

is over – this is not the time. So *shhh*, the punchline
is useless if no one listens to the docents patiently
trying to explain why we should care about orgies
being the new poetry. But for you I will try to oblige.

Matana Roberts plays *No Title* by Eva Hesse at the Whitney

A fleshlike lattice suspended from the ceiling,
orbited by bunched black taffeta and cenotaph

saxophone by way of the meanderer's swerve
that takes the shape of a heart-rending tendril.

Unbound bindings, the flayed original intent,
a final piece, uninstalled during her lifetime.

Exquisite innards, a malleable solo, a frayed
anti-heroic confronting manufactured solids,

a string sieve barely snaring latex dipped bop.
In a garb of rope that alludes to Pollock drips

a gewgaw of ghost notes confidently saunters
through a webbed net never meant to snare.

Loren Connors plays *Four Darks in Red* by Mark Rothko at the Whitney

Oxygen makes blood bright and the effects pedal
makes the electric strings hum and haw. When dry,

it's rust and clunky chords; Cha-Ching Cherry petals
boiled down to ghost notes, longer than taller. Wrong

squares on the wall of the echo chamber. A quiet slide
down the nondescript, umberish strip that seems to be

holding it all in place, through an unbroken blackout
curtain, to charred crimson tablets treading hibiscus

tea, or at least what the server told us was hibiscus tea.
Lonely crybaby learning to crawl *wah-wah* then Loren,

who, due to Parkinson's, walks with a walker and plays
sitting down, finishes by standing on his own for Mark.

Honne and Tatemae

Honne and Tatemae

after Janieta Eyre

I don't believe in the self and so self-representation is something
I think of as artifice or performance.
    – Janieta Eyre, "Auto-Interview (self-representation)"

Lonely only child, there is something
I've always wanted to ask. Do you find
it embarrassing standing nude next to
a just-met stepsister? Sorry for assuming
you're lonely, but a homesick homage
wishes for witnesses so the photographs
composed in solitude (the elaborately
cluttered fuss, painstakingly nonchalant)
mean something to someone who isn't
signified in the pastiche. At least I do.
That's why I wrote *Double Self-Portrait.*
That's why I wrote *Ekphrasis! Ekphrasis!*
That's why Nicole and I gave in to desire,
to ourselves. I discovered the photographs
of Janieta Eyre late into the writing of this
book and halfway into Nicole's pregnancy,
ashamed to have not known something
so close to what I was wanting; what I was
yearning to see. To see myself as selfishly
selfless, something like a repertoire
of responses that adjust consistency
depending on the instant. A community
drifting off together to the surf sounds
of the same seasonal sea, circadian cadence
whirring harmonically in a cicada chorus,
which is to say, there's a noise our ears
have adjusted to, normalized, assumed
to be invisible, but it's a necessary sibling
adhesive that binds at least two repetitions
together in a vague web of domestic and

the history of this twinship township is
the history of you and you, or maybe me
and me caught in rehearsal for the post-
party collapse, gawking and gagged
on the floor, regarding our reflection
in sliding closet mirror doors after guests
have left and there's no one to untie us.
"This kind of failure to speak, this kind
of terrible withholding, is something
I understand," says Eyre, someone obsessed
with doubling their body, who doesn't
panic when the time comes to shoot
the imposter, because both bodies
are imposters. The Japanese *tatemae*
(facade) obscuring *honne* (true sound),
sure, but what does true sound sound
like? The cliché is a clear bell unmuffled
by the heat from the light of morning,
smouldering through a low-lying fog,
ringing to signify something righteous.
But things rarely sound so righteous
on their own. Genuine sound skews
towards auto-interview: two same voices
simultaneously discussing themselves, softly,
so as to not talk over each other. Or a scream
echoing under a bridge that links the agony
of breathing independently with the ecstasy –
at least what you hope will be the ecstasy –
of the other releasing you like an animal;
an animal realizing that their supposedly
broken limb had never been broken at all,

it was all a terrible lie.

The Disagreement Between
Dawn and Dusk

Young Money

We want more brightness than money can imagine.
         – Timothy Donnelly, "Dream of Poetry Defense"

A poem is an attempt at learning
how to wear flip-flops with confidence

around the oddball hub where acceptance
has begun to slowly settle in. Acceptance

in the understanding that this is home now
and will remain home for as long as it takes

the haz-mat team to retard and tame the bed-
head of fibrous crystals, promising cancer,

lurking in the nooks only contractors know.
Where private money and imagination begin

to dim – childless as this space is – noon
is when first classes will start settling in.

Lesson One: exposed toes are much more
vulnerable to bloody stubs. Care for them

like a litter of hatchlings, otherwise, seeing
as there are no children here, watch out

for them with the vigilance of the young
money, who leave lights on in the hundred

rooms of this mega-mansion, ignoring
hydro bills higher than devout iowaska

decibels or burnouts hidden in the shadows
of dark parks, who've saved their allowance

to seek a new sound source, a heavy twang
with a tendril on the dimmer switch, an eye

out for subtle changes in the light, the same
old disagreement between dawn and dusk.

Stupid Machine

What you are hearing is the first music
to have been composed by an artificial
intelligence. Don't feel that you have to
hide your disappointment, the machine
is stupid and can't be hurt by opinions.

What you are hearing, believe it or not,
is an all bell work performed by monks.
It only sounds like laughter because
you were expecting laughter because
before performing the monks smirked.

What you are hearing is a reconstructed
"recording" made by sound waves vibrating
a long tool as it was used to adorn a clay vase
a thousand years ago. The artificial intelligence
read the grooves like a needle reads records,

like a laser reads CDs, like a code breaker
considers clusters of numbers. Even receipts
are trying to talk, but their voice is adding
noise to walls of noise, paper upon pavilions
of paper: park fountains in summer storms.

What you are smelling is the new carpet
off-gassing. Notice how familiar its sharp
odour is, how institutional. For a moment
try to recall all the spaces you have sat in
that make this particular tang so nostalgic –

the classrooms and showrooms and offices
that neither AI nor monk can comprehend.
When considering how to explain it to them
think of how matter-of-factly the AI reported
its interpretation of ancient ambient sound.

You were almost proud of the stupid machine –
no, don't be coy – admit it: you *were* proud
of the stupid machine whose construction
you had nothing to do with except that you
lived through it as monks live through karma

and nirvana and you changed your idea
of what a recording is (as made for playback,
because who hasn't deleted an unwatched video
of the inside of their pocket). The AI has removed
the white noise from the first recorded sounds and

what you are hearing are two monks murmuring
about their disappointment in the clay vase
they are adorning. Their voices vibrating
the long, thin tool, leaving a microscopic trail
of Braille for the blind, stupid machine to read

to future audiophiles as intelligent entertainment.
What you are touching is a tactile writing system
invented in 1824 by a blind fifteen-year-old Frenchman,
humanizing him in the "eyes" of the AI, which is itself
humanized in the video where an engineer with a bat

strikes the physical form, knocking boxes from its "hands,"
its only objective repeatedly thwarted over and over.
An emotionless Sisyphus, an expensive scapegoat
to strike and mock because it was made with a comical
voice and a ridiculous facade no engineer is afraid of.

Mine Light

When the man who built the secret tunnel
told the media that he did it to have a space
of his own, no one believed him. Before it was

a movie it was a one-act about a man hanging
caged lights on earthen walls, and before
beginning, an audience was asked to silence

their phones. Now what's passing for theatre?
Anywhere with a generator and cushioned seats.
Hush. It won't be so painful, sitting in the secret

tunnel. It's been done before, empathizing
with how far an individual can be pushed
before breaking into hundreds of shards

that refuse to consent around one another –
practising kissing with attractive contrarians,
locked jaw ajar, an unceasing gyre of brouhaha.

Go ahead and call it vapid, but it's anything
but empty crackle, the balling up of Cellophane
that hugged the box that housed habit. It's shrewd

to be afraid of naming since appropriation is all
and all is already read. Take ease in that someone
was already down here first. Shrug off any anxious

burden in exchange for blessed unrest and nullness.
Numb is the one who loses the images' personal
significance, a second chance to do over petty history

with an informal survey of friends. No, never has it
occurred to cast-off people like props after the play,
now that you mention it. Yes, most days have muttering

and occasional eating. Eating is control in a sport
that rewards those who accrue transparency towards
the light source. Self-portraiture tells us to turn off

the flash first, while sincerity rests her head on a shoulder,
whispering about past debts. When the man who built
the secret tunnel was interviewed by the famous journalist

who interviewed the whistle-blower's biographer,
the famous singer's ghostwriter, who wrote the song
about infants who refuse to keep crawling – the whole office

got up from their desks, peeked over their cubicles'
fuzzy walls, and watched it on the communal monitor
hung above the manager's always open door. A theatre

of the unimpressed performed slow claps and weak
whistles, then went back to watching whatever it was
that they watched during daylight and above ground.

Home Office

The forecast came on so fast
I hastened to grab my glass

and a few drops of precipitation
still fell in. The next sip tasted airy-

fairy, argy-bargy, other uptight-
sounding compounds as I gazed

at the storm come on like a kind
of friendship I've never known.

Sometimes taking money
is a form of friendship and

sometimes I notice the dead
moths in the moth trap by my

therapist's basement entrance
the entrance to her home office.

The weather was like this: one
week ice storms that scared us

off our last hurrah; the next, sun
like a first responder's flashlight

shined in the eyes under the guise
of checking for pupil reflexes, but

in earnest, confirming the signs
of continuation as a dull thrum

like a river or a cicada's purr
or Eli in the third trimester

letting Nicole know he was alive
by pummelling her from the inside.

The Sandbox

I wanted to do some work each day,
even if it was just holding the lid
on the box a little longer.
                    – Sarah Pinder, *Common Place*

It is said when I try I show promise
in the due diligence of the sandbox,

recognizing where the watermark
re-uploads after encryption is removed

and terminology altered. If I dreamt
about this maybe I would remember

more of it. Tiny leaves and large pollen
hovering by my half of the window

distract me. One hundred years ago
garments were sewn here. Surprising

to know how many people are up on
the roofs during most of the working

day. Choosing how to make money feels
like choosing how music makes one weep,

like how this distant figure upon the roof
chooses what litter is whipped up into

their face by the wind. But the sandbox,
the due diligence, how I think about how

I should appear while endeavouring.
No one listens to music. Exposed

pipes are insulated flash floods of other
people's shit. Sharing reluctant life with

something less than family but still more
than a malicious stranger, we will never

say we didn't give our most to be here.
But maybe later, when probation passes,

a calm can occur, an agreeable stability
that allows for other things unspoken of.

The Labour of Patience

It's true, at the moment I have some money
so I spend mornings posing as farmer or park
ranger, repopulating poems with other poems.

My lack of shame shames me; the amount
of time I spend tending to tomato plants
like I know about tending to tomato plants.

It's not so difficult to envision a next week
when I will regret writing this, when I cause
it to come apart. I was told to hold this thing

and not drop it. But I will drop it. Dropping it
is fair when field recordings fail as egg babies
and I'm not allowed to touch the thing's shards.

Shards are too sharp for a cut-and-paste man
like me. Instead, I try exit strategy fantasies.
That enough time even exists for this to be

is loose sand I push my whole head into,
listening to uncountable granules gossip
about conjugation occurring after the labour

of patience: an anticipated lightning arriving,
finally fusing them into the elegant glass circuit
that was always their inevitable, honest state.

Staff Party

By and by box two of two
will reconcile with its accomplice
and then, and only then, may the batch

be fully received, its contents counted
by an unpaid intern, a true believer
of "on order" and "on hand" commands.

Until then, fend for yourself, Guelph
veterinarian college, full of farm kids
making sense out of their childhoods'

props and costumes, sets of rolling hills:
shrugging shoulders of a giant indifferent
to the plights of those supported by parents

or who keep life alive. The old Watusi with
known unknowns and wishful thinking;
goose-pimpled cornfields and colonies

of mushrooms whose subtle presence
is but a suggestion to the islands of pines
marooned among October's crops, debris

from the new bookkeeper's beehive hairdo
she'll insist on sporting to the staff party
everyone is shucking husks from cobs for.

In Praise of Grey Spaces

Revived ravines are our laugh lines.
And by *our* I mean *we*, the costly city
whose amalgamated wards stay antsy,
playing pearl diver for years at a time.

Civic crevasses, tree-lined for people
to do whatever it is people do in tree-
lined public spaces. A capital surviving
on citizens' secrets for years at a time

like the unkillable succulent forgotten
in the attic. Did it even need you? Us?
Coyotes have come back bolder, killing
pets now. Cops shoot them off the side-

walk back to the valleys and the hydro
corridors once commuted. The gamut
and the gauntlet; the private electrical
sector. "Scars," argue some councillors,

"are made for shame and long sleeves."
So underground rivers sink heritage
buildings in the Beach, the Annex,
east Etobicoke and the wall's graffiti

is for you to see, then to be sanded
away. Before shores' sudden erosion,
a few islands provided some escape,
an open privacy of nudity previously

reserved for tax-funded public pool
change rooms. Valid bathing pavilions
with elemental acceptance and hatred
of walls. "Damn walls and not having

chickens in backyards," say some. "Let
chickens in backyards whether eaten
or not, whether the civic caress cares
or not." There's a part of the mind that

wants to have armpits, party closets
and a place to let it happen. A place
semi-private, a note quietly passed. Let
us all live as if unseen by all and as if

we only know each other because
we all signed up for the same sleep
experiment, the one where combined
inner life is municipally sneaky in deep

community gardens, doing whatever it is
taxpayers do when kiss-and-tell light is
filtered out by branch and foliage, leaving
a comfortable, collective sigh in the dim.

Counter-Earth

If we weren't hidden from one
another by the crust and mantle
or central fire, we would lose our-
selves in the gazing ball. Remember
Narcissus died satisfied and Nemesis
got what she wanted. Poetry is a lie
dummies insist is faithful. Science tries
time and time again to claim the big
narratives, but fails over and over
to boil itself down into YouTube
videos worth binge-viewing. Mass-
produced public art invokes feelings
of familiarity and there is comfort
in impossible conspiracy theories
that you and your clique believe.

Kiss Me, Man-child

As you can see from this lab coat I have on,
and by the way I speculate, I am a scientist.

Pay no attention to the Metallica T-shirt
underneath. It was my late brother's. I wear

it in honour of his great struggle. Pixelated
explosion, sad horn honk, mournful trombone

and the struggle goes on. Don't think that I was
staring at you. I was watching the silent movie

being projected over the electronic artist
during her drone set. My drug dealer calls it

"the great equalizer." My friend from uni says
he hates Shakespeare. The film shoot fubared

rush hour. I would walk, but I worked all day,
and these technicolour dream chinos have seen

enough to last an armchair creationist's rant.
After Iraq came the couscous-quinoa wars,

laissez-faire piggy banks, clown shenanigans
and ufology. This "post-racial" hug is funny

ha ha. We are both to blame for the failed
high-five. A common deafness, a thought

experiment gone wrong. People live longer
than ever and have more to say about it –

the extravagant regatta and the short-form
census no one asked for. Kiss me,

I have opinions.

Supplements

Our dogs aren't fooling anyone though they try
to speak, struggling to save the day by barking

at clues. DNA depicts wolflike hunters: Siberian
husky, Afghan hound, chow chow. All breeds

had working purpose that was lost and found
anew in laps and fenced-in off-leash areas,

impatiently waiting out a daily boredom
so solitary it spoils what we call loyalty. Royalty,

whose owners conspire to keep them alive forever.
The Queen can control corgis with her mind,

see what they see at any time, a nanny-cam world
of under beds and other butts. Nevertheless,

versions instigate themselves, extending
affection inasmuch as lives tend to braid

collectively. How impossible to break from
the domestication spiritualists shit on. Stop

procrastinating, the hill will require pragmatic
companionship, the kind where walking is still

done the day after the vet bill and procreation fails.
Best not to talk at all and endeavour to remember

who dognapped the first pup or the original wolf
who boldly stepped forward to share scraps with

those hare-brained enough to eat in the company
of animals, whose children seance labradoodles

that were left to live inside and unaccompanied
without an imagination to be bored to death by.

Dog Park

Like I've said before, I'm no Thoreau
but these dry dogwoods gesturing at
a darkening sky appear to be signalling

something unknowable only for me.
So while in this park please show me
which plants are edible, which plants

lethal. An electrical storm erratically
flashing noiseless no-nos and no
one else on these grasslands notices.

I remember one walker in this dog
park calling that a bugbear. In this dog
park beside tracks, burnt by dog paws

and drought – us owners speculated
on a train's fright, the foofaraw toted
along and looking like tortoiseshell

breadknives and aquatic dinosaur
backs. Blah, blah, blah. Then Coco
bit Luna and two adults stopped talking

to each other regarding the communal
garden. Later that Sunday, my infant son,
knee-deep in his first neurological leap,

insists on napping lung to lung,
his ear pressed against my sternum,
listening to terrified carbon dioxide

flee my body. I understand his coos
are signalling something unknowable
only for me, sincere gobbledygook

I try to reciprocate. Now I appreciate
that an escalator refusing to operate
is insisting it's an imperial staircase

and an interview is a kind
of intimacy that must fail
in order to be near to real.

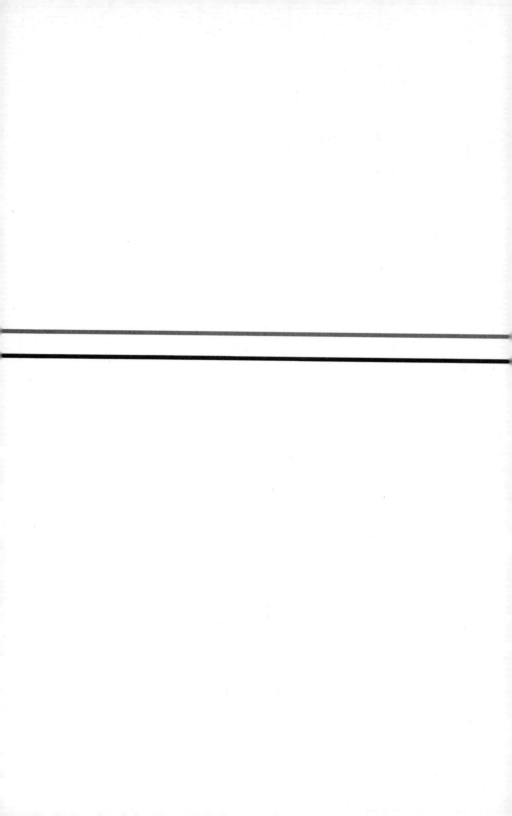

Double Self-Portrait

Double Self-Portrait

Dear Reader, earlier in this book, in the Ekphrasis! Ekphrasis!
section, which was originally its own chapbook before being

absorbed into this book, is the title poem of this book, "Double
Self-Portrait." *I wanted to make a picture...* It's based on a picture

of the same name by Jeff Wall in which he doubles himself.
As I write this I am fantasizing about using it on the cover

of this book. Did it happen? This me will never know. (Feel free
to whisper a response, useless as it is.) I can't tell you how

old I was when I first saw *Double Self-Portrait* the photograph,
but I was very young and it was at the Art Gallery of Ontario

and it's one of the first times I can remember being mesmerized.
I can tell you I didn't realize that the two men in the photograph

were the same person or that that person was the photographer.
But it was backlit and because my father taught photography,

I had already been exposed to images like this. Photographs,
but also images that made me reach to a thing I think of as affect

and I couldn't put into words. At 172 x 229 cm, it was large
and because it was backlit, it glowed like a softened monitor.

I know it was 172 x 229 cm (about 5.5 x 7.5 ft) because I looked
it up just now. But where is it? Whenever I go to the AGO I look

for it but can't find it. Perhaps it was never there, perhaps I saw
it somewhere else, or never at all. But I did see it, though I didn't

know its name. That came later. I looked it up when deciding to write
"Double Self-Portrait" the poem. I'm remembering deciding to write

"Double Self-Portrait" the poem, remembering an uncanny warmth
washing over me upon seeing the photograph after so long, knowing

I wanted to write a poem about it or based on it. I wanted to double
my memory of the warmth so I could feel it again. I wanted to return

to somewhere a long time ago at the AGO. I wanted to reawaken
to the vision of a nervous young boy mesmerized and frightened

by the image of the two stern-looking red-faced men who dressed
like his parents dressed. I just now looked at *Double Self-Portrait*

the photograph again and only one of the doubles is only vaguely
red-faced. Yet in "Double Self-Portrait" the poem I mention *red*

more than once. To me the poem is coded in red and it's "sibling"
poem, "How Does it Feel" (based on a video by Bridget Moser),

is blue. A nervous young boy who, I want to say, was on a field trip?
He was standing there by himself. Maybe lagging behind the other

students. I remember him thinking it looked like an advertisement,
the kind you might see at a bus stop. Someone could lose themselves

like that, standing mesmerized before a luminous photograph
that eclipses them. And I returned to the images – the photograph

but also the boy before the photograph, mesmerized – over and over
until I wrote "Double Self-Portrait" the poem. Now I only think of it

when I'm working on *Double Self-Portrait* the collection of poetry.
And when I'm done, I may only ever think of it when I think of my

second collection of poetry. I used to believe neglected reflections
remained in mirrors when I walked away. I used to believe everyone

had a perfect doppelgänger elsewhere in the world and if encountered,
you would have to fight to the death, because copies are uncanny

tyrants that, once discovered, drag each other down in psychic weight.
Or, as Leonora Carrington writes in her short story, "Jemima and the Wolf,"

"Isn't it enough that the world is full of ugly human beings without
making copies of them?" But by the time you read this poem my first

child will be born and I know they will mesmerize me, and, made
out of Nicole and I, will double us, continue us in a way our dog

could not. Or, as Amy Hempel writes in her novella, "Tumble Home,"
"[W]hen you have a child, your dog becomes a pet. That would not

happen to me. I can't stand the sound of a person eating, but I love
the sound of a dog crunching down on kibble ... The appetite of a baby

is a frightening thing to me." Me too, Amy. I'm afraid of the appetite for food
and the appetite for me. I worry I won't be enough, be the right person

who will only minimally frustrate them. For they will be born unfairly
sublime, a basin for impending spoil. And our dog, what becomes

of her? She will fall to the side as we side with our child, ourselves.
And the boy mesmerized before a backlit image, what does he see?

A doubled man who reminds him of his parents; a photograph
like his father has shown him; the luminescence of adulthood's

cave mouth escaping from nervousness; the glow of a red exit
sign; a shivering cicada cadence attuned to the moon before

it was explored: not mere rock – an awe unfurling, a makeshift
silk sheet pennant whose flutters physicists cross-examine

to divine the inner life of plural bodies in estrangement: an icy
sea breeze on a twinship township that composes the middle,

the time between mesmerization and learning to forgive
the fear of frustration, the fear of what I will hand down,

especially since it's all a terrible lie.

Acknowledgements
Acknowledgements

Some of these poems were originally published in *This Magazine, Taddle Creek, New Poetry, CV2, Public Pool, Train: A Poetry Journal, Really System* and *The Rusty Toque.* Thank you to the editors.

"Sunrise with Sea Monsters" was originally written for Paul Vermeersch's blog of the same name.

Ekphrasis! Ekphrasis! was originally a chapbook published by Anstruther Press. Thank you to Jim Johnstone for putting it out and for your keen editorial eye. And thank you to all the artists and writers who inspired those poems, especially Bridget Moser.

Thank you to my readers, Jeff Latosik, Vincent Colistro, Stevie Howell, Robin Richardson and Stuart Ross, for all your comments and encouragement.

Thank you to Grace O'Connell, Kevin Hardcastle, Holly Kent and *Open Book.*

Thank you to the Ontario Arts Council and the Toronto Arts Council for financial support on this project.

Thank you to Kate Trotter for all the conversations.

Thank you to Ben Estes and Canisia Lubrin for your kind words.

Thank you to Kirby at Knife Fork Book for all you do.

Thank you to Samara Walbaum and Stuart Ross (again) for all their help with the cover art. That I can have the real *Double Self-Portrait* as my cover means the world to me.

Thank you to Noelle Allen for giving me this opportunity.

Thank you to Ashley Hisson and Jennifer Rawlinson at Wolsak and Wynn for all your work.

Thank you to Alana Wilcox, everyone at Coach House Books and all the writers I've been fortunate enough to meet and work with.

Thank you to Paul Lawton, Deride O'Sullivan and everyone I've had the privilege to work with through Pleasence Records.

Thank you to Paul Vermeersch for always being interested in what I'm writing and believing in what I'm trying to do. You helped make these poems and pushed me to be a better poet.

Thank you to Nicole and Eli for making my life.

Thank you to Donald Britton for writing "Italy."

And thank you forever to Jeff Wall for making *Double Self-Portrait* and allowing its use on the cover.

səɟoИ

"The Self-Interviewing River": the line by Fred Wah that inspired this poem is "self-interviewed gutter" from "Permanent Spirit."

"Repro Ditto": the Donald Winnicott quote "The fear of domination does not lead groups of people to avoid being dominated; on the contrary, it draws them towards a specific or chosen domination" is from *The Child, the Family, and the Outside World*.

The Hissing of Sumner Lawns is an album and a song by Joni Mitchell.

"Double Self-Portrait": the italicized text is taken from "My Photographic Production" by Jeff Wall.

"How Does It Feel": the italicized text is taken from "Inside You'll Hear a Sigh" by Natasha Chaykowski, written in response to "How Does it Feel" by Bridget Moser.

"The Playthrough" and "The Playthrough" are based on YouTube Let's Play channels.

"Werewolf and Birdman": the italicized text is from *it* by Inger Christensen.

"Cranbery Bog": the italicized text is from the Wikipedia entry on Yayoi Kusama.

"Matana Roberts plays *No Title* by Eva Hesse at the Whitney" and "Loren Connors plays *Four Darks in Red* by Mark Rothko at the Whitney" are performances from the Whitney's 99 Objects series and can be found at whitney.org.

"Honne and Tatemae": the epigraph and quotes are from "Auto-Interview (self-representation)" by Janieta Eyre and from *Incarnations* (Coach House Books, 2017).

James Lindsay is the author of *Our Inland Sea* and the chapbook *Ekphrasis! Ekphrasis!*. He is the co-founder of Pleasence Records and works in book publishing